# France

**by Julie Murray**

Abdo
COUNTRIES
Kids

Abdo Kids Jumbo is an Imprint of Abdo Kids
abdobooks.com

**abdobooks.com**

Published by Abdo Kids, a division of ABDO, P.O. Box 398166, Minneapolis, Minnesota 55439.

Printed in the United States of America, North Mankato, Minnesota.

052024

092024

THIS BOOK CONTAINS RECYCLED MATERIALS

Photo Credits: Getty Images, Shutterstock

Production Contributors: Teddy Borth, Jennie Forsberg, Grace Hansen
Design Contributors: Laura Graphenteen, Candice Keimig

Library of Congress Control Number: 2023948557

Publisher's Cataloging-in-Publication Data

Names: Murray, Julie, author.

Title: France / by Julie Murray

Description: Minneapolis, Minnesota : Abdo Kids, 2025 | Series: Countries | Includes online resources and index.

Identifiers: ISBN 9798384900672 (lib. bdg.) | ISBN 9798384901372 (ebook) | ISBN 9798384901723 (Read-to-me eBook)

Subjects: LCSH: France--Juvenile literature. | Europe--Juvenile literature. | France--History--Juvenile literature. | France--Social life and customs--Juvenile literature. | Geography--Juvenile literature. | Foreign countries --Juvenile literature.

Classification: DDC 944.0--dc23

# Table of Contents

## France

France is a country in Europe. It also has **territories** around the world. Around 68 million people call France home.

France suffered great devastation in World War I (1914-18) and World War II (1939-45). The D-Day invasion took place on the beaches of Normandy in 1944. Many people visit the area each year.

US 310
Normandy
France

## Geography

France shares its borders with seven countries. France is otherwise surrounded by four bodies of water. There are also many rivers that flow through the country.

North Sea
Germany
Belgium
English Channel
Luxembourg
France
Switzerland
Atlantic Ocean
Italy
Mediterranean Sea
Spain
Andorra

France has many beautiful landscapes. It has forests, plains, **plateaus**, and mountains. Much of the country is low plains. Farmland covers about half of France.

Mont Blanc is the highest point in the **Alps**. It stands 15,777 feet (4,807 m) tall. The area around Mont Blanc is popular for skiing, hiking, and trail running.

Mont Blanc
France
Mont Blanc

## Major Cities

Paris is the largest city and the capital of France. It is the center of **culture** and business. The Eiffel Tower is a famous site. It stands 1,083 feet (330 m) high.

Paris
France

Marseille is the second-largest city in France. It is also the country's oldest city. It was founded in 600 BCE. It is a major **port** city.

France
Marseille

# Food

France is known for its breads and pastries. Croissants and baguettes are baked daily. *Boeuf bourguignon* is a French beef stew. It is often served with potatoes.

boeuf
bourguignon

## Tour de France

The Tour de France takes place in France every year. It is a 2,500-mile (4,000-km) bicycle race. Millions of people line the streets to cheer on the cyclists!

# Awesome Landmarks

Eiffel Tower
Paris, France

Louvre Museum
Paris, France

Palace of Versailles
Versailles, France

Vanoise National Park
French Alps

# Glossary

**Alps** – a large mountain range in Europe, stretching from Austria and Slovenia in the east, through Italy, Switzerland, Germany, and Liechtenstein, to France in the west.

**culture** – the language, customs, ideas, and art of a particular group of people.

**D-Day** – June 6, 1944, when the Allied forces invaded German-occupied France during World War II.

**plateau** – a high, level area of land.

**port** – a place where ships load and unload, and its nearby town or city.

**territory** – a particular area of land that belongs to and is governed by a country.

# Index